Voiceover Venture

Earning a Living with Your Voice

Table of Contents

Chapter 1. Introduction

Unleash the power within your vocal chords! In our extraordinary special report titled "Voiceover Venture: Earning a Living with Your Voice", we unravel the less trodden but promising path of professional voiceover artistry. With the rise of audio content consumption, there has never been a better time to consider this offbeat yet lucrative career choice. This uplifting guide, bustling with industry secrets, clear success roadmaps, and insider tips from established voiceover professionals, is designed to bring your hidden talent to the fore. Grab your copy, and let's launch your exciting journey into the dynamic world of voice acting as a prosperous career!

Chapter 2. Understanding the Voiceover Industry Landscape

The voiceover industry is an exciting, dynamic, and ever-changing landscape, flourishing with countless opportunities for those equipped with the right skill set, understanding, and guidance. One of the primary aspects of establishing a successful career in this field is to have a comprehensive understanding of the industry and its many facets. This chapter unravels these intricacies, laying the foundation for your voiceover venture.

2.1. Appreciating the Value of Voiceovers

Since the dawn of radio in the early 20th century, the spectrum of human voice has played a pivotal role in shaping communication. Today, enveloped by an astounding digital revolution, the demand for voiceover talents has skyrocketed. Voiceovers breathe life into commercials, video games, animated movies, television shows, phone systems, audiobooks, e-learning modules, and many other mediums.

The value of voiceovers lie in their nuanced ability to translate text into a performative medium that communicates emotion, intent, and context. Whisking listeners away on a vibrant auditory joyride, voiceovers hold the power to influence, persuade, educate, and entertain audiences. Possessing this understanding is essential for any aspiring voiceover artist, as it illuminates the inherent worth of the craft.

2.2. Broad Categories of Voiceover Work

The voiceover industry is multifaceted, bristling with a vast range of categories, each with unique demands and styles.

1. **Commercial Voiceovers**: Here, the artist promotes products or services in advertisements for TV, radio or digital platforms.

2. **Narration Voiceovers**: This includes documentary, corporate training videos, explainer videos, and e-learning modules.

3. **Promo Voiceovers**: These are employed in promotions for TV or radio shows.

4. **Audiobook Voiceovers**: The artist brings books to life through spoken performances.

5. **Animation and Video Game Voiceovers**: The artist voices characters in animated productions or video games.

6. **Dubbing or ADR (Automatic Dialogue Replacement)**: Involves replacing original dialogues with a different language or enhanced Voicing.

Each of these categories calls for a specific set of skills and styles, presenting diverse avenues for artists to explore and specialize in.

2.3. Roles & Responsibilities of a Voiceover Artist

A voiceover artist must be, first and foremost, a skilled performer. However, the responsibilities go beyond mere performance. Artists must be proficient readers, understand nuances in scripts, and demonstrate the ability to bring written words to life. They must also understand the role their performance plays in a larger context - be it a TV commercial, an animated film, or an e-book. The artist needs to grasp the purpose of the script, the intended audience, and how to best deliver the script to meet the objective.

2.4. Economic Slant of the Industry

The economic potential of the voiceover industry continues to be impressive, with annual revenues in the billions. The value comes from its wide application across countless domains like content creation, advertising, entertainment, education, and more. The thriving industry offers not just financial stability but also creative satisfaction for the talented and persistent.

2.5. Understanding the Competition

It's crucial to comprehend that the voiceover industry is marked by intense competition. With the digital revolution, artists are no longer geographically bound; one can easily compete with talents around the globe. However, with competition comes opportunity. By honing unique skills and positioning yourself correctly, you can distinguish yourself in this global market.

2.6. Continued Learning and Training

In an industry constantly swarming with fresh talent and innovations, continual learning and training are non-negotiable. Focus on improving your skill set, learn from established professionals, and seek constructive criticism. Constant refinement of skills, including diction, intonation, and acting, coupled with a thorough understanding of the industry, will help you thrive.

2.7. Importance of Networking

The voiceover industry, like any other, thrives on networking. Building a robust network will open doors to opportunities and provide valuable insights into industry trends and practices. Joining associations, attending industry events, and actively participating in communities could be instrumental in forming these essential relationships.

2.8. The Impact of Technological Advances

Emerging technologies are constantly reshaping the landscape of the voiceover industry. Artists must therefore be tech-savvy and be aware of the latest tools and software. The advent of home studios, AI voices, efficient editing tools, and online casting websites, is changing how the industry operates, offering opportunities for artists to grow and excel.

As you foray into this fascinating world, be prepared to embrace its dynamism. Continuous evolution not only in your craft but also in understanding the industry will distinguish you as a voiceover artist. The voiceover industry holds a brilliant kaleidoscope of opportunities - it's a matter of seeking, understanding, and grabbing them!

Chapter 3. Leveraging Your Unique Voice: Identifying Your Strengths

To commence your vocation in voice acting, it is quintessential to understand and acknowledge your unique voice - the one instrument that will assist you in standing out amid scores of other voices that constitute the cutthroat voiceover industry. Your voice is your indelible signature, and it is the magic hidden within this vocal brand that forms the crux of our discussion in this chapter. Here, we leverage your unique voice by identifying your strengths.

3.1. Assessing Your Voice: The First Step

Everyone's voice is inextricably nuanced and endowed with a unique character or personality. The sound, texture, rhythm, enunciation, and modulation of your voice together give it a definitive identity. To leverage your voice for voiceover artistry, start by recognizing these special and inherent traits. Record yourself while performing various tasks, such as reading a book, speaking on the phone, or engaging in casual conversation. You'll begin to detect the varying shades in your voice, how it rises and falls, how it obediently changes its timbre in accordance with your emotions. These little details will set the stage for understanding your vocal strengths and harnessing them effectively.

3.2. Understanding Your Voice Type

Depending on your tone, pitch, and overall vocal texture, you can categorize your voice into a voice type or range. The voice types are generally categorized as bass, baritone, tenor, contralto, mezzo-soprano, and soprano. Knowing where you belong could be beneficial in targeting the most suitable roles in voiceover jobs. Choose a range of scripts that best fit your voice type and practice them to perfection.

3.3. Identifying Your Vocal Strengths

While identifying your vocal strength may seem a massive challenge initially, it is one obvious way of marketing yourself in the voiceover industry. The essence lies in tone, delivery, enunciation, and pace, and their ability to captivate your audience.

Do you have a comforting, relatable tone? Or does your voice bear a authoritative, leadership-like quality? Perhaps your strengths lie in your expressive enunciation, your lightning-fast delivery, or your ability to effortlessly glide from one emotion to another while narrating multilayered stories. Once these strengths are lucidly identified, they can be bolstered to break into this dynamic industry.

3.4. Embracing Vocal Weaknesses

Paradoxically, weaknesses can turn into strengths in the voiceover realm. Every voice is filled with nuances and idiosyncrasies that may initially seem like hurdles. However, in the hands of an adept voiceover artist, these uniquenesses can morph into traits that set you apart from the sea of sameness. A voice that cracks at high pitch, a mild accent, a slow-paced delivery, could all be ingeniously incorporated into your voiceover performance, making it distinct and memorable.

3.5. Highlighting Unique Features

After identifying your strength and weaknesses, a crucial step is to highlight what makes your voice truly distinctive. Maybe it's your soothing Southern drawl, your buttoned-up British accent, or your unique ability to mimic different voices. Make these features the centerpiece of your personal branding - your unique selling proposition - and emphasize them in your voiceover demos and during auditions.

3.6. Building on Your Voice

Be consistent and persistent in practicing and honing your skills. Remember, your voice is like an instrument that needs to be finely tuned. Practice articulation, correct breathing, and voice modulation. Interact with other voice artists, observe their techniques and adeptness, and learn from their experiences. Practice narration, dramatic reading, and even singing, if it adds value to your voice range.

3.7. Your Voice and Niches

Certain voice styles fit specific niches better than others. Knowing where your voice fits best can aid you in targeting the right jobs, without spreading out too thin. Perhaps your voice carries the warmth and resonance perfect for audiobook narration, or you possess a bubbly and high-energy voice well-suited for children's content or animated characters.

3.8. Embracing Versatility

While it's essential to understand your unique vocal traits, embracing versatility is equally crucial. Yes, nurture your innate vocal style, but also challenge yourself to explore varied genres and styles in voice acting. This would widen your horizons, lay bare areas that need work, and help you become a multifaceted voiceover artist.

In closing, to optimally leverage your unique voice in the voiceover industry, a comprehensive understanding of your strength is crucial along with a persistent effort to hone your craft. Remember, it is not the sole uniqueness of your voice, but the unique way you use it that will color your journey with success in the voice acting landscape.

Chapter 4. Vocal Warm-ups and Exercises: Tuning Your Instrument

Just as an athlete would not dream of competing without sufficiently warming up their body, a voiceover artist must undergo proper vocal warm-ups to ensure their most important tool is in top condition.

4.1. Why Vocal Warm-ups?

Vocal warm-ups help to increase the circulation to your vocal cords, warming up your vocal apparatus, and reducing the risk of straining your voice. When you warm up your voice, you're essentially warming up three main parts: the vocal cords themselves, the breathing muscles, and the articulators, such as the lips, tongue, and jaw.

A regular warm-up routine can help to expand your vocal range, improve your voice's overall tone and resonance, increase your flexibility and stamina, decrease your chances of suffering vocal injury, and prepare your mind for the performance.

4.2. Singing Scales

Start your warm-up routine with a basic scale singing exercise. Ascend and descend your vocal range a semi-tone at a time. Begin in the middle of your range, then gradually work your way up, and then down, trying to add a note each end of the scale each time. This exercise will not only warm up your voice but will also start to extend your range.

4.3. Humming

Following the scales, humming is great for easing tension in your vocal folds. With your mouth closed, make the humming sound to feel the resonance, starting with low-frequency hums and gradually increasing the pitch. The objective is to feel your voice box vibrating, which can help loosen up your vocal folds.

4.4. Hissing

Breath control is key to effective voice acting, and hissing is a perfect exercise for this. It involves taking a deep breath and then releasing it for as long as you can in a steady, controlled hiss. This trains the muscles engaged in your breath support system, increasing vocal elasticity over time.

4.5. Lip Trills

Tension in your vocal cords can hinder the quality of your sound. Lip trills can be an effective method to help relax your lips and voice. Basically, you blow air through your lips, causing them to vibrate or trill together. Vary the pitch while maintaining the trill to flex different sections of your vocal cords.

4.6. Jaw Loosening

Having a relaxed jaw is vital for voice actors. Tension here may cause vocal strain, and create an unnatural or stressed sound. Place your palms on the side of your face, fingers pointing upward, and gently massage your jaw muscles. Additionally, open and close your jaws to loosen the muscles and improve diction and clarity.

4.7. Tongue Twisters

Working on your tongue twisters can increase the flexibility and agility of your speech organs like tongue, lips, and jaw. Start slowly, increasing your speed as you get more comfortable. Opt for twisters that are particularly challenging for you, as these present the most opportunity for improvement.

4.8. Cooling Down

Just as you warmed up at the outset, it's vital to cool down your voice after intensive use or practice. Repeat the same exercises as in the warm-up, but in reverse, ending with relaxed humming or gentle scaling.

It's important to remember that warm-ups are about preparing your voice, not pushing it to its limit. You're not aiming for perfection, but to simply get your vocal cords ready for the work ahead. Consistent practice of these exercises will enhance your vocal dexterity, breath control, and overall voice health, ultimately catapulting your voiceover career to unparalleled heights.

Remember, your voice is as unique as your fingerprint, and like any precious instrument, it needs to be fine-tuned and well-maintained. These exercises, when done consistently, will surely help you to 'tune your instrument' and deliver impressive voiceover performances.

However, should you ever experience persistent vocal discomfort or strain, it is paramount to seek professional advice. Do not overlook any warning signs, as any potential damage may have serious implications for your voiceover career.

Chapter 5. The Art of Narration: Technique, Tone, and Timing

Professional narration is grounded in three fundamental principles: technique, tone, and timing. Each of these components plays a significant role in the overall effectiveness of your voiceover narration, resulting in convincing storytelling that compels and enchants the listener. Gaining excellence in the art of narration requires persistent practice, constant learning, and refining your skills under these three pillars, often envisaged as the 3Ts of narration.

5.1. The Importance of Technique

Voiceover technique is a collective term for the methods and practices employed while delivering a narration. Excellent technique not just enables you to read and interpret the script effectively, but also supports in preserving vocal health.

A valuable first step on the journey to mastering technique is getting familiar with the microtechniques involved in voiceover which include speech clarity, pronunciation, enunciation, pacing, and inflection. These might sound like givens or natural traits, however, any professional voice artist would vouch that flawless execution of these parameters requires meticulous training.

Learning different breathing techniques, specifically diaphragmatic breathing, is paramount. This type of breath control empowers a sustained airflow while vocalizing, leading to longer phrases, richer tone and more efficient use of your voice.

There's also a certain degree of skill required to interpret a script. It's necessary to find the central message, spot dramatic points, visualize the intended audience, and make choices about tempo, pitch, tone, and more to create an engaging narration.

Technique is deeply tied with both vocal health and acting chops – the better your technique, the less strain on your vocal cords and the more convincingly you can deliver your lines.

5.2. Crafting the Right Tone

Tone, in the context of voice acting, denotes to the quality of your voice and its emotional context. It's an indispensable part of your narrative toolbox that can turn an ordinary narration into an extraordinary one.

Depending on the material being read, your tone may need to be authoritative, soothing, comically exaggerated, terrifying, or anything in between. For instance, a light-hearted tone would be apt for a children's book, while a documentary on climate change may require a more sober, serious tone.

The key to mastering tone lies in understanding the emotional undercurrents of a script and being aware of how tiny changes in your voice can dramatically modify the listener's experience. Once you perceive the power that the right tonal choice brings to narration, you can expand your vocal range and explore different shades of emotions.

5.3. Understanding Timing

Narration isn't just about the words being spoken, but also about the silence between them. The pacing, the pauses, and the rhythm of your speech contribute significantly to making the story engaging and real.

Good timing can make the difference between a boring, monotonous read, and a captivating, suspense-filled narrative. It helps to create tension, reveal character, and carry the listener along on a roller-coaster ride of emotions.

One aspect of timing is the pacing of your read. Too fast, and listeners may have a hard time keeping up; too slow, and they may lose interest. Audiences appreciate a variation in tempo, with significant information delivered at a slower pace and less important details sped up.

Strategic use of pauses can also add depth to your narration. Pausing can create a cliffhanger effect, emphasize a pivotal point in the narrative, or signal a change in topic or mood. Timing and pacing require a fine-balanced judgment that develops with practice and experience.

5.4. Voiceover Warm-ups and Exercises

Just like any other performer, voiceover artists need to warm up. This involves exercises to open up the vocal cords, practice pronunciation, modulate tone, and improve delivery timing.

A few effective exercises include the humming warm-up, which helps to relax the vocal cords and boost resonance. The pencil technique, where the voiceover artist holds a pencil in their teeth while reading the script, can assist in improving articulation.

Technique, tone, and timing are the foundational blocks of captivating narration. A masterful combination of these elements can leave listeners enthralled, enhancing the appeal and effectiveness of your work as a voiceover artist. It takes time, patience, and extensive practice to perfect these aspects, but the investment is well worth the rich dividends it pays in the end.

5.5. Understanding the Wider Voiceover Landscape

As we continue to dig deeper into the world of voiceover, it is crucial to understand the broader landscape. There are countless genres, styles, and applications of voiceover work, each with specific requirements for technique, tone, and timing. From audiobooks and TV commercials to corporate training videos and even artificial intelligence voice synthesis, this vast landscape widens the scope of opportunities for aspiring voiceover artists.

5.6. Market Trends and Career Advice

Even though the two main aspects - talent and technique - remain constant, the voiceover industry is continuously evolving. New technologies, changing preferences, and emerging platforms all bring new trends and growth sectors where voiceover artistry can find a thriving space.

The future holds a promising path for those who are keen on honing these triple skills and ready to step up their profession to the next level. Mastering each of these essential dimensions of narration will elevate your voiceover work above the crowd and win the hearts of listeners and clients alike.

Chapter 6. Diving into Character Voices: Animation, Audio Books, and More

The appeal of voiceover artistry lies not merely in its versatility, but also in its power to stir emotions, enliven narratives, and create characters that can be as riveting as those in live-action performances. Nowhere is this more evident than in animation, audiobooks, and other media requiring character voices. Under this illuminating lens, we delve into the riveting world of character voices - an endeavor that comes with its unique challenges and rewards.

6.1. Embracing the Art of Animation Voice Acting

Voice acting for animation is perhaps the field that comes to mind when most people think of character voiceover work. This is an avenue that offers boundless opportunities for creativity, allowing performers to bring a vast range of characters to life – from talkative squirrels and villainous monsters to sassy robots and gentle giants.

Firstly, in order to excel at animation voices, you must become adept at manipulating your vocal elements, including pitch, volume, pace, and tone. Oftentimes, you will need to exaggerate these factors to achieve the necessary emphasis fitting of animated characters. An incredibly versatile voice, capable of capturing a rich spectrum of emotions, is an asset in this field.

Voice actors must also be proficient at sustaining character voices consistently throughout an episode or an entire series. This requires significant vocal stamina, control, as well as a meticulous approach towards character development.

6.2. Navigating the Realm of Audio Book Narration

Although audio book narration may not require quite the same level of flamboyant creativity as animation, it draws heavily on voiceover skills nonetheless. Audio book narrators are responsible for creating distinct voices for all characters in a story, while maintaining a consistent and engaging narrative voice.

Successful audio book narration necessitates a strong understanding of the text. Narrators must immerse themselves in the narrative, understanding characters' subtleties and dynamics to deliver an engaging rendition of the story. They also need to be adept at voice modulation, capturing the appropriate emotion, tone, and pace for different scenarios and dialogues.

Creating distinct character voices and transitioning smoothly between them is another essential skill for audio book narrators. This requires versatile vocal abilities and an astute understanding of the human experience, bringing nuance and depth to the characters you portray.

6.3. Exploring Other Platforms: Video Games and Radio Dramas

Beyond animation and audio books, there are other arenas that envelop a focus on character voices. Video games stand out as a fast-growing industry that increasingly relies on skilled voice actors to bring in-game characters to life. Similar to animated movies and series, video game voice acting often requires unique and diverse vocal performances.

Radio dramas, although not as prevalent as they were in the past, still prevail in certain markets and continue to provide opportunities for voice actors to demonstrate their knack for character creation and storytelling through voice alone.

6.4. Mastering the Technical Aspects

While we have largely discussed the creative facets of character voiceovers, attention must be paid to the technical side of things as well. This includes understanding microphone techniques, editing and recording software know-how, and knowledge of the general production process. The importance of a professional-grade home studio cannot be stressed enough. Successful voiceover artists invest in high-quality equipment to ensure they can deliver the best possible audio quality.

6.5. Training and Practice: Your Path to Perfection

Complementing your raw talent, voiceover training is crucial to refining your skills and taking them to the next level. Workshops, online courses, and even one-on-one coaching can be incredibly beneficial. Practices such as reading out loud, mimicking other voices, and experimenting with voice modulation can help you to broaden your vocal range and capabilities.

Successful voiceover artistry depends upon a mix of creativity, technical prowess, continuous learning, and practice. As we have discovered, character voiceover work allows for the full range of human expression to be used as a valuable tool for the actor. Embrace the challenge, immerse yourself in your character, and let your voice create the magic!

Chapter 7. Building a Professional Home Studio on a Budget

The journey to a prosperous career in voiceover often begins right from the comfort of your own home. For new and emerging voice actors, investing heavily into a professional studio isn't always the most practical choice. However, with a bit of know-how, you can set up your home studio without breaking the bank. In this chapter, we will guide you through the necessary steps to establish your first home studio on a budget.

7.1. The Heart of the Studio: Your Microphone

An outstanding quality microphone is the cornerstone of a professional voiceover studio. Remember, voice acting is as much about the character and personality you infuse into your voice as the audio quality that captures it.

You don't need to splurge thousands on top-end microphones when starting. There are beginner-friendly, budget-conscious options available that do not compromise on audio quality. Some popular and proven microphone models in the range of $100-200 include the Audio-Technica AT2020, Rode NT1, and MXL 990. These mics pack a punch in performance without denting your wallet.

7.2. The Invisible Armor: Pop Filter

A pop filter, placed between you and the microphone, reduces or eliminates 'plosive' sounds. These percussive noises occur when you pronounce 'p', 'b', and 't' sounds. The damaging explosive air pressure can distort your microphone's recording, hence a pop filter is an indispensable addition.

Pop filters range anywhere from $15 to $50 with excellent options like Aokeo Professional Microphone Pop Filter and Heil Sound Windscreen for PR30 & PR40 available. It's an affordable investment to ensure pristine audio quality.

7.3. The Sound Keeper: Headphones

A pair of high-quality, closed-back headphones is crucial to pick up any little nuances in the audio that may need correction. It aids in getting the audio levels right during recording and helps to identify any background noise, plosives, or clipping.

The Audio-Technica ATH-M30x and Sony MDR7506 Professional Large Diaphragm Headphone are two budget-friendly yet high-quality options. They will set you back by around $70-100, but the investment is invaluable to uphold professional standards.

7.4. The Sound Barrier: Acoustic Treatment

The echo and background noise can wreak havoc on your recording quality. To combat this, your recording space needs acoustic treatment. Foam paneling, bass traps, and diffusers can help control sound reflections and remove any unwanted noise.

Foam paneling is a cost-effective solution for a home studio. A 12 pack of 12"x12"x2" soundproofing panels can cost as little as $20, and with creative placement, they can significantly improve your audio quality. Bass traps and diffusers are slightly pricey but can help to take your studio's acoustics to the next level.

7.5. The Nerve Center: Computer and DAW

Your computer and digital audio workstation (DAW) software are the main hub of your studio operations. You'll need a reliable and relatively quick computer to handle the audio recording, editing, and rendering tasks. You probably won't need to buy a new computer unless your current one is unusually slow or outdated.

For DAW software, the free Audacity software is sufficient to start. As you progress, you might consider upgrading to more professional software such as Adobe Audition or Pro Tools, both of which offer more advanced editing features. The cost of these softwares can range from $20-$50 per month.

7.6. The Lifeline: Audio Interface

An audio interface carries the important task of converting the analogue sound of your voice into the digital format your computer can understand, and vice versa during playback.

Behringer U-Phoria UMC22 and Focusrite Scarlett Solo (3rd Gen) USB Audio Interface are good quality equipment which can cost between $50–$120, and they are more than enough to meet the needs of a start-up home studio.

7.7. Piecing It Together: Cables and Stands

Getting the right cables to connect your microphone to your audio interface is equally important. A wrong cable can degrade the sound quality. XLR cables are the industry standard for microphones and deliver superior sound quality. A reliable cable can cost you around

$10-$20.

The microphone stand keeps the microphone set at the correct height and angle, freeing your hands for scripts and other controls during recording. The Heil Sound PL-2T Overhead Broadcast Boom and Heil Sound FL-2 Flange Mount are excellent low-budget yet sturdy choices ranging from $25–$70.

Investing in a home studio is not about buying the priciest items. It's about understanding your needs and prioritizing them effectively. At the end of the day, your talent and skill will supersede any high-end equipment. Be wise with your purchases, invest in quality over quantity, and spend not beyond your means. This beginner's studio will serve its purpose perfectly while you hone your skills and establish yourself in the voiceover industry. Thus start your venture with a budget-friendly setup and upgrade as your career progresses.

Chapter 8. Developing an Impressive Demo Reel

The journey to becoming a professional voiceover artist invariably leads to creating an impressive demo reel - a showcase of your inimitable vocal talent and versatility. When put together expertly, a demo reel can be a compelling testament to your breadth of skill, acting as the linchpin in your quest to secure voice acting opportunities.

8.1. Building a Repertoire

Begin by laying the groundwork needed to record your demo reel. Prepare a varied selection of scripts that suit your voice type and will allow you to show your range. A well-rounded list may include scripts from commercials, video games, films, animation, documentaries, and audio-books. Try to avoid clichés and embrace diversity in your selection.

Select texts that allow you to demonstrate a wide variety of emotions and tones. For instance, you might want to show your ability to wield a soothing, educational tone for documentaries, and also a playful, dynamic voice for animation.

8.2. Studio Quality Recording

Use a quiet, sound-proof space to record your scripts, to eliminate any background noise that can disrupt the quality of your recorded voice. To add a professional touch, consider investing in a quality microphone that provides clear, detailed audio recording.

Your recording environment plays a significant role in capturing pristine audio. A professional or home studio with proper acoustic treatment is ideal. This doesn't necessarily have to be prohibitively expensive - portable vocal booths or even a well-prepared closet can work if you're on a budget.

Remember, the quality and layout of your audio indicate the level of professionalism and effort you put into your work, sending a strong message to potential clients about your commitment to your craft.

8.3. Voice Control and Acting

Once you have a collection of scripts and a suitable recording environment, it's time to bring the scripts to life. Read aloud, focusing on the texture and tone of your voice.

Speaking clearly and accurately is one cornerstone of voiceover work, but there's another equally important aspect — acting. When recording your demo reel, inject each piece with believable emotion and character to bring the text to life. Demonstrating your acting abilities can set you apart and shows directors that you're not just a voice, but a performer as well.

Listen to professional voiceover samples, observe how they deliver emotions and characters, and try adding your unique twist into your performance.

8.4. Post-Production.

The post-production phase is where you'll polish your recordings into a compelling reel. Here, you can remove any undesirable noises or pauses, control any volume disparities, and ensure all your tracks have uniform levels.

Music or sound effects can also be a great addition to your demo reel, granting it an extra layer of professionalism, but use them judiciously and make sure they don't overpower your voice.

You could do the editing yourself using an editing software, or hire a professional audio engineer. If you want to DIY, consider learning how to use audio editing software like Adobe Audition, Audacity, or ProTools.

8.5. The Structure of Your Demo Reel

The sequence of the scripts in your demo reel matters. Typically, you'll want to put your strongest piece first as it would grab the listener's attention right from the start. Then, weave a mix of different tones and styles from your script repertoire.

Keep your demo short, ideally between one to two minutes. Remember, a casting director might be sifting through hundreds of demos, so ensure yours stands out and keeps them interested.

8.6. The Value of Feedback

Feedback is the key to improvement. Seek advice from mentors, voiceover communities, or established voiceover artists and incorporate their constructive criticism into refining your reel.

The road to a prosperous voiceover career is both demanding and rewarding. Though the process of crafting an impressive demo reel might be complex, it's an investment that can secure your path in this dynamic industry. Don't rush the process, take time to develop your skills, and you'll find the end product is worth the investment.

Chapter 9. Marketing Yourself in the Voiceover Industry

Launching a successful career in the voiceover industry requires more than just talent. You need to know how to market yourself so that potential clients are aware of your existence and skills. Here's a comprehensive blueprint to help you create your voiceover brand, reach potential clients, and build lasting relationships.

9.1. Building Your Voiceover Brand

Every successful voiceover artist has a unique brand that encapsulates their voice style, delivery, and character. Branding begins with understanding your strengths and figuring out your unique selling proposition (USP). As a voiceover artist, your USP is the distinctive tone, emotion, or trait your voice brings. Whether it's the ability to mimic various accents, deliver high-energy narration, or recreate soft, soothing tones, it's these elements that make your voice unique.

Once you've identified your USP, reflect it in every aspect of your marketing material – from your business cards to your website and online profiles – to create a cohesive brand image.

9.2. Creating a Voiceover Demo Reel

Your demo reel is a critical tool for marketing in the voiceover industry. It serves as a showcase of your vocal range and acting skills. Your demo should include different types of reads – commercials, narrations, phone prompts, cartoon voices, etc. – that are various in tone, tempo, and style, displaying your versatility.

Investing in professional production for your demo can make all the difference; a high-quality demo can help you land potential clients. However, if budget constraints are a concern, you can create your own demo at home with suitable recording equipment and sound editing software.

9.3. Building Your Online Presence

In our fast-paced digital world, having an online presence is crucial. Set up a professional website showcasing your voice-over demos, past work, testimonials, and contact information. Optimize the site for SEO to increase your visibility on search engines.

Utilize social media platforms – LinkedIn, Twitter, Facebook, Instagram – to reach out to potential clients and engage with your audience. Sharing your work, offering voiceover tips, engaging in discussions, all of these help to establish your online presence.

Participate in voiceover forums, attend industry events (virtually or in person) and join online groups to network with others in the industry.

9.4. Pitching to Potential Clients

Once you've prepared your marketing tools – a brand, a demo, and an online presence – you'll be ready to reach out to potential clients. Research companies that hire voiceover artists like advertising agencies, production houses, and e-learning companies. Customize your pitches and convey how your voice can enhance their project.

Persistence is key. Don't become disheartened if you initially receive more rejections than positive responses. Keep refining your approach based on the feedback received.

9.5. Building Long-Term Relationships

Long-term client relationships are built on trust, reliability, and delivering quality work consistently. Always deliver your projects on time, follow your client's directions to the letter, and be ready to make necessary changes to meet their expectations.

Keep your clients updated about your new work, share your updated demo reels, and connect with them on special occasions. Such gestures help in maintaining connections.

As important as it is to gain new clients, remember not to overlook your existing clients. Satisfied clients are likely to refer you to others, thus fueling word-of-mouth marketing, one of the most potent marketing tools.

9.6. Continuing Education and Improving Skills

Stay relevant by continually updating your skills. Attend workshops, take up courses, get professional coaching. Not only will these widen your skill set but they will also add credibility to your profile. Furthermore, share your learning journey on your online platforms to show your dedication to your craft.

By implementing these strategies, marketing yourself in the voiceover industry can be an exciting, rewarding process. It's certainly a commitment that requires time, effort, and a bit of strategic planning. But, with persistence and perseverance, you'll be able to craft a unique brand for yourself, expand your network, attract potential clients, and ultimately, turn your voiceover passion into a rewarding, profitable career.

Chapter 10. Establishing Your Network and Mentorship

Just as how a captain in the middle of an ocean relies on his compass and charts, in the field of voiceover artistry, relationships and guidance become your navigational tools on your journey. They provide you with the direction to steer your career in the right direction. This chapter will help you understand the importance of establishing a feasible professional network, nurturing healthy relationships, and seeking beneficial mentorship in the voiceover industry.

10.1. Building Your Network:

A network is more than just a list of contacts. It's a web of relationships that can provide opportunities, support, advice, and more. To start building your network in the voiceover industry, begin with the following steps:

1. Attend industry events: Every event is a unique opportunity to meet potential contacts. Many important industry figures attend these events, and you might have the chance to interact with them.

2. Join industry organizations: Organizations that cater to voiceover artists and industry professionals are excellent platforms. Membership offers various benefits including networking opportunities and continual learning prospects.

3. Participate in online forums and communities: The internet provides several forums and groups where you can interact with experienced voiceover artists and learn from them.

4. Collaborate on projects: Working with other professionals can help to establish stronger connections and foster long-term

relationships.

When networking, remember that it's not about self-promotion at the expense of others. Rather, it's about sharing and gathering information, seeking ways to be of service to others, and developing mutually beneficial relationships.

10.2. Using Social Media for Networking:

In the digital age, social media platforms allow you to network on a global level. They are easy to use and offer numerous possibilities to connect with professionals and industry insiders.

1. LinkedIn: A professional networking site loaded with individuals who are serious about their craft. It offers exposure to potential clients and collaboration opportunities.

2. Twitter: Following relevant hashtags like #voiceover or #voicetalent can connect you to the trends and people within the industry.

3. Facebook: Many voiceover groups are available for both beginners and professionals, providing a space for discussions, collaborations, and sharing of opportunities.

While using social media to network, always remain proactive. Share your work and achievements, interact regularly with other members, and offer your supports when necessary.

10.3. Building a Professional Relationships:

No man is an island, and this holds true in the voiceover industry, too. It's not only about what you know but also who you know.

Professional relationships don't come about in a day but are formed over time through trust and mutual respect.

1. Be professional in your approach: Always present yourself professionally, even in informal situations. This helps to establish your credibility.

2. Don't hesitate to ask for help: It's a common fear that asking for help shows a lack of competence. However, a willingness to learn and grow is well-regard in any industry.

3. Always be sincere: Authentic relationships are built on sincerity. Be genuinely interested in other people and they will reciprocate that interest.

10.4. Seeking and Choosing a Mentor:

As a beginner in the voiceover industry, you will find a mentor's guidance indispensable. The right mentor can provide insights based on their experience and can guide you in making the right decisions.

To find an appropriate mentor, it may be most effective to:

1. Know your needs: Understand what guidance you require. This will help you to identify the skills that you should seek in a mentor.

2. Do your research: Familiarize yourself with the notable professionals in the industry, and learn about their careers and experiences.

3. Approach them directly: Once you've chosen a potential mentor, make your intentions clear and respectful when approaching them.

Remember, the primary purpose of having a mentor is to grow and learn. Always be open to feedback, seek advice regularly, and make sure to express your appreciation for their time and efforts.

10.5. Utilizing Your Mentor's Guidance:

Having a mentor is one thing, but using their guidance effectively is another. It's essential to know how to maximize your interactions with a mentor:

1. Be clear about your expectations: Let your mentor know what you aim to accomplish in your conversations. This will help you both make the best use of your time.

2. Be open to criticism: A mentor's feedback, even if it seems harsh, is a tool for improvement if applied effectively.

3. Implement their advice: No matter how valuable their guidance might be, it will be useless if you don't take action based on it.

This chapter has given you a foundation on which you can start to build your network and seek mentorship in the voiceover industry. These tools, when used effectively, can dramatically improve your chances of success. Always remember, as an old adage goes, "Your network is your net worth," and it certainly holds true as you venture into the vast world of voice acting.

Chapter 11. Sustaining and Scaling in the Voiceover Business

Achieving success in the voiceover business requires a combination of-talent, capitalizing on unique opportunities, and consistently raising your game to keep pace with the evolving industry. However, success is just the first step on your journey. Beyond that, you have to figure out ways to sustain the momentum and scale your operations for continued growth and profitability. In this chapter, we'll explore the strategies that can help you stay ahead of the competition, leverage resources, and secure a long-term career in the ever-changing voiceover business.

11.1. Laying Foundations for Enduring Success

Sustaining success in your voiceover career is all about laying the right foundation. As you begin to experience a modicum of prosperity, reflect upon what brought you there in the first place. Keep a keen eye on your unique selling propositions - it might be your distinctive voice, your multilingual skills, your ability to switch between characters, or perhaps your unmatched delivery speed. This will help you identify the niches where you excel and should focus on for sustainable growth.

Building a professional network is another critical aspect of a strong foundation. Be it voiceover agents, other talent, or editors; these are the people who will keep you informed about new opportunities and industry developments. Attend industry events, join online communities and forums, and don't hesitate to ask for assistance or offer your help to others.

11.2. Nurturing Relationships for Repeat Business

As you know, a significant part of the voiceover industry is driven by repeat business. Clients often prefer to work with familiar voices that they trust can deliver high-quality work. Keep your clients satisfied by consistently delivering excellent output and responding to their needs promptly and professionally.

Remember, every interaction is a chance to demonstrate your worth and build a lasting relationship. Send regular follow-ups, thank you notes, and occasional gifts to show your appreciation. This thoughtful approach will not only bring repeat business but also increase the likelihood of garnering referrals.

11.3. Investing in Continuous Learning and Improvement

The world of voiceover is dynamic, with shifting trends and technological advancements constantly presenting new challenges and opportunities. Therefore, continuous learning is crucial to staying relevant and competitive.

Participate in voiceover workshops, webinars, and training sessions offered by industry experts. They provide valuable insights on various aspects such as new delivery techniques, handling difficult scripts, and ways to maintain vocal health.

Embrace new technology. From noise-cancelling microphones to recording software, having the right tools can vastly improve the quality of your work. Stay updated about technological advancements related to voiceover and equip your studio accordingly.

11.4. Diversifying Your Portfolio

Consider diversifying your portfolio to further scale your business. You might be excellent at commercial voiceovers, but there's an entire world to explore - audiobooks, animated shows, video games, e-learning, and much more. Each domain requires a different skill set and style, providing a learning curve and various paths for growth.

Additionally, a diverse portfolio showcases your versatility and increases your potential customer base. Agencies and clients are often more inclined to work with a voiceover artist capable of handling a range of assignments.

11.5. Exploring International Markets

Once you've established a strong footing domestically, consider branching out to international markets. With the rise of global platforms, reaching a worldwide audience has never been easier. Not only will this boost your earnings, but will also provide you with global exposure, leading to more opportunities and experiences.

Remember, going global means adjusting to different languages, accents, cultures and legal stipulations. Try to develop a basic understanding of the market you're venturing into.

Further, localizing your marketing efforts can go a long way. Have multilingual versions of your website, demo reels, and marketing materials to attract non-English-speaking clients.

Lastly, don't forget about self-care. As with any self-employed venture, it's easy to work round the clock, but remember to take breaks and maintain a work-life balance. Your vocal cords are your treasure; keep them healthy.

The journey to sustaining and scaling your voiceover business might be challenging, but as long as you keep your passion alive, continuously learn, and adapt to the environment, the sky's the limit for your success.